The Chamber of Commerce

Provo: The Garden City of Utah

Its Resources and Attractions

The Chamber of Commerce

Provo: The Garden City of Utah
Its Resources and Attractions

ISBN/EAN: 9783337100612

Printed in Europe, USA, Canada, Australia, Japan

Cover: Foto ©ninafisch / pixelio.de

More available books at **www.hansebooks.com**

PROVO:

THE

GARDEN CITY OF UTAH.

ITS : RESOURCES : AND : ATTRACTIONS.

PUBLISHED UNDER THE AUSPICES OF

The Chamber of Commerce.

1888.

D. C. DUNBAR & CO., PUBLISHERS.

OMAHA, NEBRASKA.

THE TABERNACLE.

PROVO.

EARLY HISTORY.

ESTLING at the base of the Wasatch Range, where its deeply seamed front towers high and precipitously toward the sky, lies Provo, the "Garden City" of Utah. The pioneers of Utah entered the Great Salt Lake Valley in the fall of 1847, and in the following spring a small party from this body started south on an exploring expedition. Immediately on reaching the summit of the divide, between what are now Salt Lake and Utah Counties, they gazed southward, and beheld stretched out before them, calm and undisturbed, a beautiful sheet of water some thirty miles in length, hemmed in on all sides by towering peaks, with yet enough of plain to tempt the settler, and with many streams pouring out from rugged ravines, threading their silvery way through the uncultivated area until lost amid the sleeping waters of the lake. Roaming along the banks of these rivers in search of game, and about the shores of the lake, was a tribe of Indians who possessed the spot as their own. They were the "Utes," though the opinion of some is that they properly should be called "Pah Utes," or "Water Utes." The fact seems to be that not only this lake and Utah County, but even the territory, ultimately derived the name "Utah" from this tribe, and that "Piute" county is only "Pah Ute" corrupted, or improved, as we may choose to think.

Be this as it may, the exploring party, satisfied with the inviting appearance of the spot, reported favorably, and a party soon started south to colonize the newly discovered section. An agreement was made with the Indians by which the pioneers were permitted to locate in the new valley, and a fort was built at a point a short distance below the spot where the Denver & Rio Grande Railway track now spans the "Timpanogas" River.

Accessions to the new settlement caused an extension of its borders, and, as circumstances permitted it, the tendency seemed to be to go closer to the mountains on the east. Ultimately the first site of Provo or "Utah Fort," was abandoned, and the city built a little further away from the "Timpanogas" River, which now supplies Provo with water.

How the place came to be called Provo, is not an absolutely settled point; but the more plausible explanation, and that

PROVO WOOLEN MILLS.

most generally credited, is found in the following story: General Fremont, on his first exploring trip to the Pacific, passed through this valley when returning eastward. Before leaving the Missouri River on his journey westward, the General bought a fine blooded animal from a Frenchman named "Proveau." This animal carried him to the shores of the Pacific and as far as our valley on his return, when it sickened and died. The "Pathfinder" had become greatly attached to the horse, and named the spot where it was buried after the animal itself, it having been known by the name of the Frenchman from whom Fremont had purchased it. The other theory is that "Provo" is so called after an old mountaineer and trapper who made the valley, the border of Utah Lake, and the course of the "Timpanogas" River the scene of his periodical hunting and trapping visits.

The word "Timpanogas," signifies "rushing water," or, putting it more graphically, "rocky torrent," or the tumultuous rushing of water over a rocky bed.

COURT HOUSE AND CITY HALL.

The early history of Provo, if written, would be devoted in the main to a recital of extreme hardships, resulting from bitter and almost incessant Indian wars. While the pioneers of that place were permitted to establish themselves by a friendly arrangement with the red men, it did not long continue. The Indians soon began a characteristic and most violent warfare upon the hardy settlers. In founding this now fruitful and prosperous locality, not a few of the best men were killed. It

was practically a continuous struggle, with brief seasons only
for the pursuit of agriculture. But as the early settlers had
gone there to stay, and were possessed of that courage which
is characteristic of the men who settled this territory, the
locality prospered and grew, notwithstanding the Indian depre-
dations and the loss of many able men in the predatory warfare
which the Indians so persistently maintained.   There is left,
it is true, little or no trace of the struggles through which this
thriving city was founded; and only occasionally, as the mind
of some veteran reverts to earlier days, do those now enjoying
the peace and prosperity which prevail here, realize, even in

TERRITORIAL INSANE ASYLUM.

the most distant sense, how dearly the blessings by which
they are surrounded were purchased.   Pleasant it is, and
sweet, to behold these cultivated fields and numberless homes
where the people dwell in comfort, surrounded by the luxuries
of modern times; but few there are who can appreciate the
extent of labor that has been performed to bring about the delightful results which everywhere in this valley charm the eye.
But if the thoughtful will pause and consider through what
struggles these results have been achieved, the sense of ad-
miration for the persevering toil of those who founded this
prosperous commonwealth must overshadow all other feelings
and leave little room for other sentiments than those in which
reverence for the pioneers predominate.   It is impossible to

estimate the extent of wealth contained in the canals and ditches by which the fruitful acres of this valley are watered. How slowly, and with what excess of unyielding toil, these were built, only those who participated in the work can realize. The wealth, not only of this valley, but of our whole territory, is represented more in its canals and irrigating ditches than in any other direction—perhaps more than in all other directions combined. Millions of dollars in the hardest coin—the honest sweat of honest men—have been spent in canals; and those

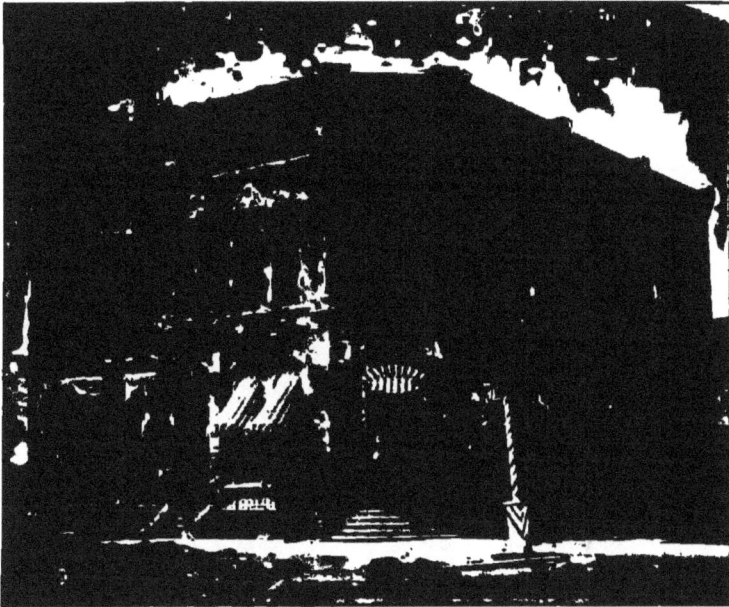

FIRST NATIONAL BANK.

who live to-day, who prosper and enjoy comforts that, without these canals, would be unknown here, can never fully sense how great is their indebtedness to those who fought and worked, who worked and fought, that this county and this city might be.

THE CAPITAL OF UTAH COUNTY.

Provo is the capital of Utah County. This county is second in population in Utah. The city is surrounded by one of the richest agricultural sections in the whole territory; there being settlements continuously north and south of it, and around the western base of the Wasatch Mountains 'or a distance of some

forty miles. The people are prosperous. and unitedly strive to
promote, as well as participate in a growth which is now quite
rapid, not only in the city, but also in the entire county. Being
the first born of the county, and its capital, Provo has naturally

PROVO CENTRAL SCHOOL.

been built up more rapidly and more solidly than its neighbors.
The population of the city is between 5,000 and 6,000.

  It is a peculiarity of this place, that all who make it their
home, become thoroughly and substantially identified with it,
working unitedly for its prosperity and progress.

RESOURCES AND OPPORTUNITIES.

  If Provo is so favorably situated as a place for the building of a home, it is no less desirable as a locality for the invest-

ment of means and for the establishment of manufacturing
enterprises. Surrounded by boundless resources, prominent
among which are almost limitless agricultural opportunities
which lend substantial aid to the mining investment, the mar-
vel is that comparatively so little advancement has been
made, situated almost in the heart of the Territory, considered
as to population, and nearly in the centre geographically,

PROVO OPERA HOUSE.

Provo is rapidly being viewed as the coming seat for manufacturing in Utah. Its fitness for the position is the more pre-
sumable from the fact that no other point along the western
base of the Wasatch, situated as near the centre in trade and
population, possesses equal facilities either in the matter of
power for operating manufactures, or in the abundance of resources easy of access and upon which industries may be
founded.
Unlimited manufacturing opportunities once conceded, the
next point in connection with the growth of manufacture in

this section is the ease with which ingress and egress may be obtained by means of railroads for the exportation of the goods manufactured, for the supply of coal, and if it be necessary, for the inbringing of raw material. That Provo is blessed with these advantages in abundance will be clearly shown in this pamphlet.

S. S. JONES' MERCANTILE ESTABLISHMENT.

WATER POWER AND SUPPLY.

In an economical sense, the chief feature of Provo is its opportunities for the founding of manufactures. Its water power, extending a distance almost of seven miles without diminishing the force of the stream, or interfering with its utility for irrigating purposes, is inferior to none in the Rocky Mountain Region. The "Timpanogas" is a constant and unfailing source of industrial power, and scarcely any limit can be placed to the possibilities it presents for the operation of

any number of manufactures that may be built upon its banks.
It is already the site of the largest Woolen Mill Manufacturing establishment in the west,—the "Provo Woolen Mills,"—
and the marked success being achieved in this branch of local
industry, points emphatically to the assured prosperity of
other industries, on equal scale, when the needed capital is in-
vested in the many other directions for which the locality is so
eminently fitted.

It may also be well to add that in recent years the sinking
of artesian wells has been introduced with results astonishing-
ly successful.   There seems to be no limit to the subterranean
reservoirs over which, not only Provo, but Utah County gen-

PROVO LUMBER AND MANUFACTURING MILLS.

erally is located; and what is more striking still, is the fact
that, on the average, these wells require to be sunk less than
200 feet in order to obtain a good supply of water, almost un-
excelled for its purity and admirably adapted both for culinary
purposes and for irrigation.   Another interesting feature in
this connection, is the fact that there is no perceptible diminu-
tion in the water in wells already in existence by the sinking
of new ones. It is, therefore, reasonably inferred that practically no limit can be placed to the supply.   Arrangements are
now making for the sinking of a huge well on the elevated
plateau north of the city, by Denver parties; and the persons
interested are so confident of success that the securing of
water means to them simply a matter of the time necessary

to sink the required depth. These wells, as before stated, being valuable for irrigating purposes, there can be no reasonable probability of a time coming when there will be a lack of water for all purposes in and about the city of Provo. As to the quality of the water supplied by the Timpanogas River, it need only be said that a brighter, a purer and a clearer stream is nowhere to be found. Distributed over the fields, running through the charming "Garden City" in countless uncovered streams that adorn either side of each street and afford moist-

THE NEW WEST SCHOOL.

ure for the shade trees everywhere abounding, it gives a freshness and a perennial delight peculiar to few other cities in the world, outside of Utah.

IRON ORE.

In Utah County, not far from Provo City, are situated vast iron fields capable of furnishing millions of tons of ore for the manufacture of iron, so free in its nature that it is used as a flux in the smelters of Salt Lake Valley. This will yet find labor for thousands of people and bring in return millions of dollars annually to the territory, and to this city and county more particularly, when the day arrives that Utah iron receives the attention which its magnitude merits. There has

been incorporated in Provo a company known as "The Utah
Valley Iron Mining and Manufacturing Company," its present
officers and board of directors being John E. Booth, president ;
Walter R. Pike, vice-president ; Wilson H. Dusenberry
treasurer ; A. O. Smoot, Jr., secretary ; A. A. Noon,

SNOW BROTHERS' FURNITURE EMPORIUM.

superintendent.   These, with Amos D. Holdaway and
Thomas Beesley, constitute the directors.   The company
proposes soon to begin the manufacture of iron.   The
property owned consists of large bodies of iron ore,
situated on the east hills of the Tintic Mining District,
less than thirty miles from Provo City.   The company's
possessions extend over a tract of land of some 340 acres, and

contain, one might almost declare, absolutely inexhaustible
quantities of ore which is found in dykes or deposits. These
are twenty-six in number, but their depth or width has never
been ascertained. For the purpose of mining, or, rather, quarrying the ore, it is only necessary to clear off a light covering
of earth, and then proceed as in rock quarrying, with powder

MRS. E, HORTON'S STORE.

and drill; and a single blast will very often tear down a hundred tons. The fronts of ores thus exposed are, in many in-
stances, nearly a hundred feet high from the floor of the
workings to the top; but this is not the depth of the ore, for
even the floors of these quarries are of solid iron ore and of
the purest quality, reaching down into the earth to unknown
depths. Wherever shafts have been sunk for the purpose of
prospecting, the ore has improved in quality with the depth.

attained. Developments have been made in these deposits by means of hundreds of feet of excavations, tunnels and cuts, all of which expose such quantities of ore that it would be difficult, if not impossible, to name a place where they are rivaled in extent or in excellence of quality. Under the conditions stated, the working of these ore bodies is very light in expense. The road to the mine is of easy grade; single teams can be driven to and from any part of them, and haul 4,500 pounds to the load, while two railroads are but a few miles distant.

EXCELSIOR HOUSE.

IRON AND BRASS MANUFACTURES.

It should be stated here also that the largest operating company for the manufacture of machinery and the working of brass and iron in Provo city, is the "Provo Foundry and Machine Company," of which an organization was effected in January of 1886. The present officers are H. H. Cluff, president; J. E. Booth, secretary; and John Devey, superintendent. The main building occupied by the works of the company is 80x32 feet. It is two stories high and is built of adobe and brick. A commodious molding room in the rear of the building is 60x40 feet, besides engine rooms and shops which are usually constructed with such works. The company has all the latest and most improved machinery--planers, turning

lathes, power drills, and furnaces necessary for brass and iron
casting, and the baking of cores for hollow iron works, with
wide capacity, and facilities which do not include those used
in the manufacture of machinery. At present, but a limited
number of workmen are employed by reason of the heavy
cost of pig iron now imported from the east. This difficulty
will, however, be overcome at no distant day, as the company
heretofore mentioned, which has in its possession the largest
iron beds in the country, but a few miles from this city, con-
template the erection of furnaces for the manufacture of pig
iron as soon as possible. The foundry company has been

RESIDENCE OF JUDGE W. N. DUSENBERRY.

thoroughly successful in its work, and is daily turning out
machinery and castings fully equal to those produced by eastern institutions of a like kind.

IRON FIRE-PROOF PAINT.

The manufacture of fire-proof paint, though still in its in-
fancy, has already attained considerable importance in Provo.
The idea of the manufacture of paint from iron ore was first
suggested to Mr. A. A. Noon, of Provo, by the large quantities of ore thrown aside as waste, for the reason that it was
considered not of the best quality for fluxing rebellious ores
at the smelters. The iron ore possesses a beautiful red color,
and a little over a year ago experiments were made to manufacture it into paint by crushing the ore to small particles and

then mixing it with oil. This, when applied to woodwork, was found to give a bright, rich color; but the powder was not sufficiently fine. Many difficulties were experienced and were only overcome after numberless experiments and at a great outlay by the Provo Foundry Company. By a novel and original method the ore was reduced as fine as the finest flour and the cost of manufacturing the paint reduced to a minimum. As soon as the article and its merits grew to be known, there came demands from all parts of the territory for it; and the machinery which, when built, was deemed equal to supply the trade for years, was found to be altogether

RESIDENCE OF DR. W. R. PIKE.

inadequate. Other and larger machinery was built and, in another year, still greater facilities will be imperatively necessary. The manufactured article is brown or red, and is not only largely fire-proof, but is most excellent for its preserving qualities in changeable climates. Wherever it has been used, it is pronounced to be far superior to the eastern article. The ore from which the paint is manufactured is from the deposits owned by the "Utah Valley Iron Mining and Manufacturing Company," in Tintic mining district, already referred to.

UTAH GRAPHITE.

A fine quality of graphite, or black lead, is mined near Payson, Utah County. The mine is owned by the Provo

Foundry Company. The ore is found on an incline vein several feet in thickness. So far as developments have been made, the ore improves in grade with the depth attained. At present, it is used only as foundry dusting, in the molds into which the melted iron is run and its effect is to produce a smooth surface which could be secured in no other way. No very extensive experiments have been made with this article, for the reason that the capital of its owners has been used in other directions ; but with proper working and treatment, it will certainly become a valuable article of commerce in Utah, and soon be among Provo's important industries.

RESIDENCE OF DR. JULIUS HAMBERG.

WOOLEN MILLS.

The largest and most successful woolen mills in the West are located at Provo. The excellence of the goods manufactured grows yearly. Being in the centre of an immense wool growing district, it has every opportunity, and the success of this institution demonstrates that others have only to enter the same field, display like energy and business tact, to reap the same gratifying rewards. There is not a doubt that Provo could support manufactures capable of working $2,000,000 worth of wool annually. The extent of the workings of the Provo Woolen Mills is evidenced in the facts here given, which were furnished by its superintendent, Mr. Reed Smoot.

The Provo Woolen Mills Company own a full block of ground in the heart of the city upon which the mills stand. The mills are run by two Turbine wheels, to each of which there is eighteen feet of water pressure. The main part of the building is 75x145 feet in dimensions, adjoining which is a room 15x33 feet. Running at right angles with the main building, while south of and adjoining the room just mentioned, is still another two-story structure, 33x134 feet. The main building is four stories in height. There are in the mills, wash rooms, bins for storing the wool, eight sets of carders, three carders to a set; grinders to keep the carders in trim;

INTERIOR VIEW OF DR. JULIUS HAMBERG'S LIBRARY.

a spooler and reel, and a jack with 240 spindles for making yarn; there are also four self-acting mills, 125 feet long, each having 720 spindles; two machines for spooling the thread; thirty-seven narrow looms for flannels; nineteen broad ones for cassimeres and blankets; one warp dresser, one shawl fringer, and a spooler and beaming frame for arranging the warp. A fire pump, with a capacity of 300 gallons per minute, together with piping through all the works, with fire plugs and hose, are the protection which is afforded against fire. Moreover, the mill possesses three fullers, three washers, two gigs, two presses, two cutters or shear frames, and two brushes, one with and one without steam.

The mills have manufactured nearly 500 designs since the

day they began operations, in the fall of 1873. The capacity
of the looms is over 1,000 yards per day, and 1,000 pounds of
wool is consumed each day. Fully 5,000 pounds of soap is
used weekly for cleaning the wool ; and since last spring over
$12,000 has been spent in dye colors. Every year sees an in-
creased demand in the goods, this demand, outside of the
home consumption, coming from Montana, Washington, Idaho and Wyoming Territories, and the States of Nevada, Colorado, Minnesota, Michigan, Missouri, Louisiana, and, in fact,
from almost every state and territory in the Union.

It is the largest woolen mill west of the Missouri River,

RESIDENCE OF DR. F. H. SIMMONS.

and is incorporated for $500,000, in shares of $100 each. Though
having a hard struggle in the beginning, with excellent management it is doing remarkable work to-day, and promises
even better for the future.

LUMBER MANUFACTORY.

Large lumber mills, which commenced some years ago,
and which are situated in the immediate neighborhood of the
Utah Central and D. & G. Ry. depots, supply all classes of
woodwork for Provo, and places not only in the county, but
at great distances. In fact, it is almost safe to say that not
a single industry of a manufacturing character has been started that has not met with success, in view of which fact it is

surprising that more extensive work has not been undertaken.

ASPHALTUM.

About sixteen miles east of Provo, on the line of the Denver & Rio Grande railway, are situated the asphaltum mines of the "North American Asphalt Company." There are thirty-three claims, covering an area of nearly 640 acres. The vein is from eight to fourteen feet in thickness, and lies almost horizontally. It is the only pure asphaltum in the United States. There are other small discoveries in the vicinity, but none suitable for paving, nor any of the uses to which asphaltum is put. The latest developments have uncovered deposits containing from 40 to 60 per cent. pure asphaltum. The company is a St. Louis organization. Adolphus Busch, the wealthy St. Louis brewer, and president of the Anheuser-Busch Company, is its president, and among the stockholders, officers and directors are such men as Phillip Stock, H. P. Taussig, and Charles Nagle. St. V. Le Seiur, the discoverer of the deposits, is manager and superintendent. The company is now erecting machinery, costing $25,000, for working the ores. The building will be three stories high and 114 long by forty feet wide. It will be capable of working 100 tons every ten hours, and will manufacture everything possible from paving material to the finest varnish. Already nearly $20,000 has been expended in prospect work and experiments. The company is incorporated for $1,000,000.00 and will, beyond doubt, be a signal success, a benefit to the county, of the greatest value to Provo City, and of material profit to our territory.

MANUFACTURING POSSIBILITIES.

It may be worthy to note here some branches of industry and manufactories which promise immediate and gratifying returns upon operations being undertaken, and for which Provo seems singularly adapted. Among others are the following:

STOVE WORKS.

In this connection it may be said that there are no stove works west of the Missouri River. At least half of the cost of a stove in the inter-mountain states and territories is that of

freighting. With iron works established, and with the limitless iron resources already mentioned, the manufacture of
stoves, grates, etc., upon a large scale, would be a source of immense and immediate profit. The market afforded is an
extensive one, comprising Utah, Western Colorado, Idaho,
Montana, Wyoming, Nevada, Arizona, California, Washington Territory, Oregon, and even the east.

CANNERIES.

Utah County is the largest fruit producing section between
the Rocky Mountains and the Coast. Vast quantities are
shipped to Colorado and surrounding states and territories.
There is no doubt that a fruit canning establishment upon an
extensive scale would pay handsomely. Moreover, the canning
of other agricultural products is equally possible. The tomato
in Utah County is a safe crop. Every condition seems to pro-
pitiate its growth, and its size and rich flavor both recommend
it as an article that, canned properly, would soon rival and
perhaps overshadow in the east and west the famed Utah po-
tato. In this direction alone is an extensive field for enterprise,
and when we couple with it the richness and size of the Utah
peach, plum, pear, strawberry, raspberry and grape, it will be
discovered that in the United States there is no unutilized industry in the same direction that rivals Provo in the promises
held out to enterprise and capital.

PICKLE AND VINEGAR WORKS.

Pickled cucumbers and onions are imported into Utah and
sold in the Provo market. Better cucumbers and onions are
raised nowhere in the world, while apples, from which the very
finest vinegar can be made, lie rotting on the ground and are
fed to cows and pigs because a market is not offered for them.

ROLLER FLOUR MILLS.

Utah County, with Sanpete, Millard, Juab, Sevier and other
counties south, of which Provo is the natural key, produce
wheat in the greatest abundance. Large roller mills would
receive the great surplus of wheat shipped to other sections,
and would pay a handsome profit on investment. They would

find an extensive local market, and a territory east and west into Colorado and Nevada and far south.

BEEF PACKING.

This county and others are filled with herds of cattle, the greater part of which are marketed outside of the territory. An enterprise of the kind indicated would be a source of immense income to the inaugurators, and would find a virgin field. That Utah should have no beef packing establishment, pro-

HON. A. O. SMOOT.

Hon. Abraham O. Smoot is one of the representative men and pioneers of Utah. He was born in Owen County, Kentucky, on the 17th day of Februray, 1815. He joined the Church of Jesus Christ of Latterday Saints in 1835, and traveled in the ministry for about a year and then went to Kirtland, Ohio. In the spring of 1837 he returned to Kentucky and in company with H. G. Sherwood organized a company of Saints and led them to Far West, where the Saints had located after being driven from Jackson County, Mo. He continued in the ministry until the latter part of 1838. Was taken prisoner at Far West when that city (which was held by Mormons) fell[1] before the forces of the milita of the State and the mob. While a prisoner he married his first wife, Martha T. McMeans, on the 11th day of November, 1838.

When the Mormons were driven from Missouri in February, 1839, he left with them, suffering many privations in the inclement weather, and arrived at Quincy, Ill., March 8th. He spent the spring months there. From there he moved to Nauvoo and went forth again into the ministry. In the Exodus of the Latterday Saints across the Plains and Rocky Mountains to Great Salt Lake Valley he led a company of 120 wagons, sharing the privations and hardships of the dreadful journey with a fortitude that illustrated his character and determination.

In 1851 he went on a mission to England and on his return conducted a large emigration to Salt Lake City. In 1856 he was elected Mayor of Salt Lake City by the City Council to fill the vacancy caused by the death of J. M. Grant, the first Mayor of that city. In Feb. 1857 he was elected Mayor by the unanimous vote of the people at their regular election. By repeated elections he continued in office until February, 1866. His wise and conservative policy advanced greatly the progress of the city. Declining the mayorship in 1866, he served twelve years in the Council branch of the Legislature. In February, 1868 he went to Provo and was immediately elected mayor of that city. He served Provo twelve years as Mayor without any remuneration whatever, just as he served as Mayor of Salt Lake, without salary. He is President of the First National Bank, Zion's Co-Operative Mercantile Institution, the Lumber Company and the Provo Manufacturing Company.

He has ever worked to advance Provo and Utah County, and has been the financial backbone of its business institutions since his connection with the County, over which he stands as spiritual head, being President of the Utah County Stake of Zion. A man of mighty strength and resources, the hard experiences he has undergone and the labors of the past have made him a monument of worth in the region which he has aided to reclaim from a desert and transform into a garden dotted with the homes of men, who now honor and respect his name.

ducing the beef it does, and surrounded by a beef producing area as it is, is one of the surprises that await the stranger.

SHOE FACTORIES.

Nearly all the hides produced here are shipped to points outside, made into boots and shoes and returned to be sold. We pay freight on our own hides both ways, that they may be returned in a shape to be worn. That the margin will not justify the manufacture, is absurd, especially in view of what has been done in Salt Lake in the same direction. No argument is needed to show that the manufacture of these articles within the territory would find ready and profitable markets.

In addition to the industries specially mentioned, there are many others that would justify an extensive investment. Among them, without exhausting the list, we may mention:

CHEESE FACTORIES.—For butter is a drug at 15 and 20 cents per pound.

A TANNERY.—For what is said regarding shoe factories applies here.

CRACKER FACTORY.—A market unsurpassed in the west is offered such an enterprise.

AGRICULTURE.

HOP CULTURE.

Some three years ago, Major Berry, who is owner of a large tract of land on the bench, just north of Provo, made some experiments in the culture of hops; and while considerable difficulty was experienced in the beginning, the results attained during the season just past have been of the most gratifying nature, and have demonstrated, beyond the peradventure of a doubt, that this very important and desirable industry is thor-

HON. W. H. DUSENBERRY.

The present Mayor of Provo, Wilson H. Dusenberry, is one of the leading men of Utah county, and is to-day, perhaps, one of Provo's most useful and generally utilized citizens. He was born April 7th, 1841, at Perry, Pike county, Ill. He is the younger brother of Warren N. Dusenberry, Judge of Utah county. Mayor Dusenberry was reared in his native State. In 1860, with his father's family, he went to California, visiting Provo on the outward trip. After being in California for two years, the brothers returned to Provo, where, out of respect to their mother's wishes, they remained and became identified with the introduction of a systematic and higher education in that city, out of which has grown the present advanced state of educational institutions in Utah. He was County Superintendent of schools from 1874 to 1880. Wilson Dusenberry began his political record in 1872, when he was elected a member of the Provo City Council, with which he has been associated ever since, (excepting for a part of 1874-5) as Councilor, Alderman and Mayor. He was County Clerk from 1875 to 1883. In 1879 Mayor Dusenberry was elected a member of the House branch of the Utah Legislative Assembly. In the same capacity he served in 1882 and 1884, being a member for three consecutive terms. He was the most prominent member in that body in securing the adoption of the parliamentary rules which still obtain. In 1882 he was chairman of the House Committee on education and in the Territorial Convention that nominated Hon. Jno. T. Caine as delegate 'to Congress, he was made President. In 1864 Mayor Dusenberry married his cousin, Harriet V. Coray, the niece of the late Delegate, Wm. H. Hooper. She died, leaving two child-dren, in 1872. In 1874 he married Margaret T. Smoot, daughter of Hon. A. O. Smoot, of Provo. He is and has been since its inception cashier of the First National Bank of Provo. Mayor Dusenberry is quiet and undemonstrative, clear sighted, possessed of marked political ability and business sagacity, and, is one of those men whose influence has been felt throughout the entire Territory.

oughly practicable in this locality. It is a new undertaking in Utah ; and because the soil and locality seemed peculiarly adapted to the culture of hops, Mr. Berry was induced to make the experiment. On this bench, also, there is good reason to believe it is the purpose of eastern capitalists to establish large fish ponds, as the water from artesian wells seem specially suited to this purpose.

GROUND PRODUCTS.

Moreover, all the land on this bench enjoys the breezes which forever come down Provo Canon ; and the value of these winds to fruit-growers is inestimable. The frosts of early spring, in many quarters, destroy the fruit crops by nipping the tender buds; but wherever there is an unfailing breeze, the frost is carried about and, not being permitted to settle on the buds which may be shooting out, they are protected and the season's fruit crop is assured.

The soil, also, is a fine sandy loam ; and because of its natural warmth is well suited to the culture of grapes. The canon breeze is also of great benefit in this respect ; and the gentle slope of the land being to the west, it enjoys the warmth of the afternoon's sun. The result is, not only fruit of the most luscious description, grapes large and of rich flavor, but also vegetables that are of rapid growth and of early maturity, The soil bears all the lighter cereals and vegetables. Potatoes and onions are particularly famous, and hundreds of car loads of the first named are exported annually, the demand coming from parts as far distant as Cincinnati and New Orleans.

Celery, asparagus, and garden vegetables of all kinds are cultivated and grown in great quantities. Small fruits abound, and the grape, if repetition may be forgiven, is of as fine flavor as the celebrated California product. It is dark and rich in color, large in size and delicious in quality, and is grown extensively throughout the valley. Apples, plums, and apricots are raised in large quantities. The climate and soil are particularly favorable to the culture of peaches, and nowhere in the world are finer ones raised than in Utah. They are universally conceded to be superior in every respect to the peaches

HON. H. B. CLUFF.

Harvey Harris Cluff, son of David and Elizabeth Hall Cluff, was born January 9th, 1836, in Kirtland, Ohio, being the seventh of a family of twelve, whose ancestors came to America shortly after the landing of the Pilgrims and settled in the "New England" States, some of whom served as Legislators, officers and soldiers during the struggle for independence, his father being in the war of 1812.

David Cluff became a convert to the doctrines taught by Joseph Smith and moved to Springfield, thence to Nauvoo, where the family remained until the Exodus in 1846, when they located at Mount Pisgah, thence they went to Musquito Creek, Iowa, where they remained until 1850, at which time they crossed the Plains to Salt Lake and located in Provo in October of the same year and joined in completing the "log-fort" and school house. In the spring and summer Mr. Cluff tended his father's flocks along the base of the Wasatch mountains, improving every opportunity of his shepherd life by studying the Bible, Book of Mormon and Doctrine and Covenants. In the winter of 1854-5 he lived with his brother David, at Parowan, and in 1856 volunteered, on the 6th of October, to a call of President Brigham Young, to aid the late Hand-Cart companies across the Plains. The following day he started from Salt Lake City in company with 40 men and 22 mule-teams loaded with provisions and clothing. It was on the Sweetwater, near the South Pass, where he aided in saving two men from freezing to death. The last of that season's emigration was found at the upper crossing of the Platt. Heavy snow storms caused delays at Devil's Gate, preventing their arrival in Salt Lake until the middle of December. The experience of this trip is beyond description. On the 24th of January, 1857, Mr. Cluff and Margaret Ann Foster were united in marriage, to whom four children were born, all dying while very young. He was elected City Councilor in 1859 and in the following year, with three brothers, built a large furniture factory and music hall. In 1862 he was elected a City Councilor and re-elected in 1864, serving until 1865, when he went to Europe as a missionary, laboring six months in England and two years and a half in Scotland as President of the Glasgow Conference, and the last year over the Scottish District, returning home in 1868 leading a company of 400 Saints. One year afterwards he went to the Sandwich Islands accompanied by his wife. He returned thence in 1874. He obtained a clerkship in the Provo Co-Operative for three months, served as manager of the Utah County *Times* Publishing Co. two months, and in 1875, by appointment, commenced the duties of Assessor and Collector of Utah County. He continued in that office until 1879. In August, 1875, he was ordained by President Brigham Young, Bishop over the Fourth Ward Provo. He was again elected City Councilor in 1876, and in 1877 he was called into the quorum of the Presidency of the Utah Stake of Zion with A. O. Smoot and D. John. In 1879 he was called to preside over the mission on the Sandwich Islands, and went, accompanied by his wife. There he erected a sugar mill at a cost of $24,000, and commenced a meeting house 35x65, returning home in 1882. For several years after his return he superintended the Provo Lumber Manufacturing and Building Company and has been superintendent of the erection of Utah Stake Tabernacle from its beginning. On the 20th of September, 1883, his wife died in Provo City. In the beginning of 1884 he was elected President of the Provo Theatre Company and in 1886 made Director of the first National Bank of Provo. He has yet many useful years before him.

of either Delaware or California. The trees here are of much hardier growth and less subject to the blasting influences of the frosts than elsewhere.

THE GARDEN CITY.

Provo is very properly designated the "Garden City." It is the fashion in these days to have a high sounding sub-title or name for every city almost in the country. In most cases these names have but little, if not a painfully ridiculous signification, and are mostly the result or wish of the over-confident and ambitious citizen. Provo, however, is justly entitled to its second name. It is deservedly called the "Garden City" of Utah, and the valley, in which it lies like a gem, might rightly be termed the garden valley of the west.   The soil is rich, and the climate of the most favorable kind for the production of that which pleases equally the mind, the eye, and the palate.   It is the home of the vegetarian, where this philosophic individual could live and feast the year round, and the spot of all others to be favored of an epicure.

SCHOOLS AND CHURCHES.

The city is laid out with wide, handsome streets, at right

JUDGE W. N. DUSENBERRY.

Warren Newton Dusenberry was born in Whitehaven, Luzerne County, Pennsylvania, November 1st, 1836.   His mother's parents were prominent people in that part of the state.   Mahlon Dusenberry, the father, moved from New Jersey to Pennsylvania where he married Aurilla Coray, the mother.   The Dusenberrys are of Holland descent, but on both sides the families are of long American ancestry.   The mother was a great granddaughter of Abigail Green, sister of General Nathaniel Green, one of the most noted commanding generals of the American Revolution.   Judge Dusenberry is the third child in a family of nine children.

In 1840 his family, with his grandfather Coray's family, emigrated to Pike county Illinois.   In 1860 they crossed the Plains going to California with ox and horse teams.   On this trying and hazardous journey the principal burdens rested upon Warren N., who was then twenty-four years of age.   Late in the fall of 1862 they returned to

Utah and located at Provo, where with his brother Wilson II., he soon became the leading educator at least of Utah County. He and his brother are not only practically the founders of the school system in Provo, but also are to be credited largely with the founding of the Brigham Young Academy there. He followed the vocation of teaching most of the time until 1874, when he was elected by the Legislative Assembly Probate Judge of Utah County—an office he still holds. During the time since 1874 Judge Dusenberry has been a practitioner at the bar of the District Courts of this territory as well as the Supreme Court of the United States, besides holding numerous other positions of trust and honor. Prominent among these, and one which will ever be a monument of honor to his name, is his connection with the Territorial Insane Asylum. His sympathetic sentiments for the distress of his fellows impelled the drafting of the bill which became the law creating this institution. To him more than any one has been accredited its location at Provo and its present advanced state. For more than five years he has been President of the Board of Directors, and most of the time chairman of the executive and building committees. With Dr. Pike he made a tour of inspection among the asylums of the United States for the information which has helped to place Utah's asylum on a much higher plane than any similar institution in our inter-mountain region. Judge Dusenberry is a conservative man and has exercised great influence in Utah County in bringing it to the front and giving it the prestige it now enjoys.

angles to each other, and attractive public buildings are not wanting. Schools were among the first structures that were thought of by the early settlers, and from the first adobe room built, the system has grown until now, Provo has a complete and most excellent school system. · In regard to these advantages, the Garden City perhaps leads the territory; and with two academies, and its public schools, will compare most favorably with the east. Churches are not lacking, and the utmost freedom of worship, thought and action prevail. All the blessings attendant upon civilization elsewhere are found in Provo; and one can live there surrounded with the same culture and refinement as in older and wealthier cities east or west.

It is conceded that Provo has the best district school house in the territory, recently erected at a cost of $20,000. The foundation is also laid for the Brigham Young Academy, the cost of which, when completed, will not be less than $75,000. The new Northwest Educational Association has also erected a fine building here, known as the Proctor Academy, at a cost of $8,000. There are a number of other school houses, new and commodious, which would swell largely the aggregate amount this thriving city has put into institutions for the education of its young.

One of the finest buildings in the territory is the Tabernacle in Provo. It has already cost close on $75,000, and when all work is done on it, will not run under $100,000. Besides this there are a number of lesser church buildings, as well as Presbyterian, Methodist and other edifices for the worship of God, which give the city a metropolitan air, and offer a variety of forms of worship for those who are not particular where the Sabbath is observed.

HON. S. R. THURMAN.

S. R. Thurman was born May 6, 1852, in La Rue County, Kentucky; received an academic education; moved to Utah in 1870, and at once commenced teaching school at Lehi City, Utah County, which vocation he followed almost exclusively for eight years. He then began the practice of law, and went to Ann Arbor, Mich., 1879, attending the law lectures for several months at that place.

He is associated in his profession with Mr. George Sutherland, a firm which, without doubt, has the largest and best practice of any south of Salt Lake City. Mr. Thurman commenced official life at the early age of twenty-two. From that period to the time of his going to Ann Arbor he was an Alderman and member of the City Council of Lehi City, and in 1882 was elected Mayor of that place, an office he resigned when moving to Provo in November of the same year. He was a member of the House of Representatives of the Utah Legislature in 1882, being the youngest member of that body, and was recognized as one of its ablest members. He was returned in 1884, 1886, and is a member of the present Legislature, where his influence is second to none. In 1882, together with Hon. John T, Caine, Hon. P. H. Emerson and Governor Arthur L. Thomas, he was appointed to revise and codify the laws of Utah. He is at present, and has been for some years, County Attorney for Utah County and Attorney for Provo City.

Politically he is identified with the history of the Territory. He was a member of the Constitutional convention of 1882, and also of the late Constitutional Convention which framed the anti-polygamy constitution. He was chairman of the committee which drafted the first declaration of principles or platform of the People's Party, and delivered the first political speech in the first political campaign of that party in 1882. Of his National politics, he is a pronounced Democrat. Mr. Thurman is a man of growing capacity and is one of Utah's prominent lawmakers and politicians.

PUBLIC BUILDINGS.

The Territorial Insane Asylum is located at Provo. After going through several counties in the territory seeking for an eligible site for the building, the committee, having the selection under control, chose the site now adorned by this building. A portion of the structure, the south wing, is completed, at a cost of $120,000. It is supplied with all the modern and most approved appliances, is surrounded by a beautiful tract of land for farming, is built right under the overhanging Wasatch peaks, and commands a glorious view almost of the whole valley and of the lake on the west. When completed it will cost not less than half a million dollars.

The County Court House and City Hall, a joint building, cost $30,000, and occupies a valuable site. Now in course of erection and almost completed, is a new County Jail, built after the most modern architecture, with steel cells and a pleasant and attractive exterior, which will cost $15,000 to $18,000.

Perhaps no other city of double its population in the United States has so fine a building of amusement as Provo. The Provo Opera House has a seating capacity of 900, and cost over $30,000. Like all other public institutions in Provo, everything is new and contains all the modern advantages in the line for which it was erected. It may be unnecessary to state that a city with such a building has a good record among traveling theatrical companies for the number of its amusement-loving inhabitants.

There are several hotels in the city which, while not of a pretentious nature, nevertheless afford ample accommodations, and all supply a most excellent table.

The First National Bank of Provo occupies a building that cost over $20,000. The Bank was organized and began operations in 1882, with a capital stock of $50,000. It has paid 10 per cent. dividends from the beginning, and has a reserve fund aggregating 11 per cent. of the capital. Its stock is to-day worth 1.10. The above facts are based upon the institution's report of October 5th last, in which also it was shown that nearly $3,000 undivided profits were on hand, in addition to the reserve fund of $5,000. The officers of the Bank are: A.

DR. W. R. PIKE.

Walter R. Pike, M. D., was born in Norfolk county, England, on the 8th of June, 1848. He came to the United States alone at the age of sixteen years, having previously spent some time at sea. After traveling for three years in the western country and putting up with the inconveniences and roughness peculiar to western life in earlier days, he settled down to the study of medicine in Salt Lake City, being then nineteen years of age. Under Dr. J. S. Ormsby he studied for two years; then he entered the drng business, pursuing that vocation for over five years and until he obtained a most thorough knowledge of drugs and medicines. He then went east in 1876 and graduated from the medical department of the University of Vermont in 1877. From here he went to New York City, entering the University of New York, from which he graduated in 1878, taking the two degrees in as many years. He then returned to Utah and located in Provo, where he began the practice of medicine and has remained there continuously ever since, excepting one year of practice in Salt Lake City. He preferred the former place, however, and returned there, where his practice and influence have grown together. He has held for several years the position of county and city Quarantine physician, but resigned both upon being appointed Medical Superintendent of the Territorial Insane Asylum, which is located at Provo and which was opened in 1885. The Doctor is advanced and yet conservative in his ideas, is of a very progressive turn and has won a wide reputation and been more than ordinarily successful.

O. Smoot, president; Wilson H. Dusenberry. cashier; with a directory of strong and trustworthy men. There is ample room and a most excellent opening here for at least one other bank. One hundred thousand dollars to $150,000 could be safely invested in this direction.

Being so centrally located, with so many advantages, there is one thing that is surprising to the inquirer and the business men—the absence of jobbing houses equal to the opportunities the city affords. One large wholesale house. which must have cost all of $30,000, stands near the depots of the two railroads. The signs are that Provo will soon occupy the position as a jobbing centre, which its geographical situation undoubtedly warrants. Provo's legitimate market is the whole of the southern, eastern and western parts of Utah and of Western Colorado—all mining and growing agricultural areas.

CITY OFFICERS, NEWSPAPERS, CHAMBER OF COMMERCE.

Provo is a chartered city, and has been one for many years. Its present officers are: Mayor, Wilson H. Dusenberry; Aldermen, A. O. Smoot, Jr., Walter Scott, W. H. Brown, J. E. Booth; Councilors, Roger Farrer, Charles D. Glazier, Evan Wride, Wm. McCullough, David Holdaway, John M. Holdaway, Joseph T. McEwan and James A. Bean.

The "Utah Enquirer" is the oldest paper in the county. It is a semi-weekly; the "American" is of recent birth and issued weekly. Besides these, which are newspapers, are the "Utah Industrialist," a monthly magazine, and the "Home Circle," a literary periodical.

The Chamber of Commerce, under whose direction this pamphlet is published, was organized in September last. To-day it has a membership of sixty, and is second to none in the territory in the effectiveness of its work, in the unity of its members and in the determination with which it pushes to

completion any policy that may be adopted as the sense of the
Chamber. Its officers are : Wilson H. Dusenberry, president;
James Dunn, first vice-president; A. A. Noon, second vice-
president; who, with S. S. Jones, Reed Smoot. W. C. A. Smoot,
Jr., F. H. Simmons, Richard Brereton, W. R. H. Paxman and
Joseph A. Harris, constitute the directory. George Sutherland
is secretary, with Ed L. Jones, treasurer.

DAVID JOHN.

David John was born at Little New Castle, Pembrokeshire, South Wales, January
29th, 1833. He was the son of Daniel John and Mary Williams. His father was an in-
fluential farmer. His parents were members of the Baptist church, many of his family
being ministers of that denomination. It was designed by the family that John also
should be educated for the ministry; and for this purpose he spent four years in the Baptist College, Haverford, West South Wales. He became identified with the Church of
Jesus Christ of Latter Day Saints on the 6th of February, 1856, and is still a member of that body. On the 6th of April, 1861, he sailed in the ship *Manchester*, from
Liverpool to New York, arriving in Salt Lake City in September of the same year,
whence he went direct to Provo, and has since resided there. He has spent years in the
ministry of his church, abroad and at home. He has combined business with religion,
for he has been a school teacher and a business man in the Provo Co-Operative Institution; in the Provo Woolen Factory, and in the Lumber Company, which originated
with the firm of Smoot & Johns. He left the factory to fulfill the duties assigned him
in the church. He served as one of the trustees of the Provo district schools for fifteen

years, and for as many years he has served as a member of the Board of Directors of the Provo Co-Operative Institution. He is now in the prime of life, and gives promise of still being of much use to his church and his country.

PROPERTY VALUES AND TAXATION.

The city property is assessed at $721,863, which is about one-fourth of the fair cash valuation. On this amount for city purposes, six mills on the dollar are assessed, making the tax, on an actual cash valuation, only one and one-half mills on the dollar. The county taxable property is placed at $3,386,000, which is about one-third of its cash value. The territorial, school, and county tax on the assessed valuation, amounts, in all, to eleven mills on the dollar, which brings the actual tax down to three and two-thirds mills on the dollar. The municipal, county, school, and territorial taxes, the total on an actual cash valuation, aggregates therefore, but five and one-sixth mills on the dollar. On this showing there need be said no words of commendation. It tells its own tale.

RAILROADS.

Both the Utah Central and the Denver & Rio Grande Western Railways run through Provo City. The former is run in connection with the Union Pacific, and is practically one of its branch lines. It extends some 200 miles south of Provo, and makes this city the supply quarter, largely, for Southern Utah. From the south, all wool passes through Provo to local points, before being exported east, and a vast amount of it finds a home market at the Provo Woolen Mills already referred to. Provo is the junction of the Denver & Rio Grande Western Railway with the Utah Central. It is also the nearest city of any importance to the boundless coal fields, situated some sixty miles distant, near the main line of the Denver & Rio Grande Railway, in what is known as "Pleasant Valley."

There is absolutely no limit to the coal supply; and with this considered, in connection with the colossal iron deposits heretofore mentioned, it gives a solid character and reliability to the prediction already made, that Provo is destined to become the seat of immense manufactures; especially for the production of crude iron, if nothing be said of the numerous branches that necessarily follow upon the production of pig iron.

It is important to note in this connection that south of what is known as the "Weber Pass," through which the Union Pacific now runs, there is no really practicable route for a new railroad (and the number that are now rapidly rushing to Utah from the east may not be counted on the fingers of one's hand), until Provo Canon is reached. This gives foundation to the prediction that several through lines from the east are destined to come to Provo; and, as other cities of magnitude east of Provo are impossible, because of the unfavorable conditions of

S. S JONES.

Samuel Stephen Jones, one of the founders of Utah County commerce, (and at the present time a prominent merchant of Provo City), was born at the Angel Inn, Brentford, England, in February, 1837.

Mr. Jones obtained his business experience with the firm of Bardsley & Son, Tea Merchants, Tottenham Court Road, London, which was also a post and money order office. He came to Utah with the never to be forgotten Hand-cart Company, in 1856. After passing through for several years the harsh vicissitudes of early western life, he engaged in business with Messrs. Birch & Stubbs, of Provo City. Later he embarked in the mercantile business himself. He took a leading part in establishing the Co-Operative movement in Provo, and acted as superintendent of the Provo Co-Operative Institution for several years. Mr. Jones' present business is second only in Provo

City to the Co-Operative Institution. Besides his store at Provo, he has a branch establishment at Price, Emery Co., and conducts also the business of charcoal burning at his kilns in Spanish Fork Canyon from which the Germania & Hanauer Smelters, in Salt Lake Valley are supplied.

Of his public service it may be noted that he was Adjutant in the Provo militia; assisted in raising supplies and forwarding troops to San Pete and Sevier during the Indian campaign of 1862, and accompanied Col. Nuttall with a company of men to the Sevier. He has been in the City Council several terms as Councilor and Alderman. In fine, S. S. Jones for many years has been in various spheres a representative man in the Provo commonwealth, and a pillar of its commercial fabric, as he is to-day.

the country lying there, it necessarily follows that, the importance of Provo as a railroad town and a manufacturing centre is necessarily and incalculably enhanced.

ATTRACTIONS.

At the base of the Wasatch range of mountains, and at a point where its peaks rise abruptly, reaching upward until their tops seem almost to pierce the sky, lies the manufacturing centre of the coming State of Utah. It is about four miles south of a mountain canon of the same name as that of the city. Through this canon the Timpanogas River, or the river of "Stony Waters," as the Indians graphically name it, dashes its course, until, in spreading through numerous artificial arteries and veins, it pours upon the teeming acres that lie between the mountains and the pleasant bosom of Utah Lake. The high embankment north of the city forces the river to sweep in a semi-circle to the south and west. The river is thus thrown above the city, and gives ample supply for all the purposes of manufacture and for irrigation. Along its course have grown up beautiful groves, interspersed with fruitful fields and pleasant meadows. In and around there are lovely and quiet drives and lanes, with wild roses, flowers and shrubs growing in rich profusion.

The Utah Lake is on the west of the city. It is the largest fresh water body in the west, and can be reached in a twenty minutes' drive. The view from any point—north, south, or east—only lends fresh charm to the effective scene. Into the bosom of the lake pour the waters of the American, Timpanogas, and Spanish Fork Rivers, and its outlet is in the Great Salt Lake, through the Jordan River. The city, during the summer, is clothed in a complete verdure of fruit, ornamental

and shade trees.   The lay of the city, with its broad and level
streets, as seen from the mountains, afford a soft and pleasing
vista.   Through the trees the main buildings of the city can
be seen, and off to the west slopes a stretch of fruitful farming
land with its contrast, in regularly laid out fields of yellow and
of green.   The lake spreads out from this latter point, and the
opposite range of mountains on the western side of the valley,
breaks the view, forming a fitting background for a scene of
such pastoral loveliness.   The mountains are famous for their

A. A. NOON.

The life of A. A. Noon has been one of many strange scenes and circumstances.
He was born in Middlesex, England, on the 28th of June, 1837.   His father was a
professor of languages in London; was educated in Gottenberg, Germany; served in
the Prussian navy and finally settled in London, where he practiced his profession.
A. A. Noon left London for New Orleans, when but a boy, in 1851 at the time of the
great excitement in California.   From America he went to Australia at the time of the
great rush to the gold fields, and with that wave went to Ballarat, Bendigo, and other
noted mining sections.   There he prospected and worked in the mines, and was reasonably successful.   He went from Australia to India and was at Calcutta at the time
of the excitement because of the massacre at Delli.   From India he went to England
again; thence to Africa, where, in connection with his brother, Adolphus H. Noon, he
helped to establish, among the first, the sugar enterprise of Port Natal, and owned,
by rental, the Ispingo estate, a farm of one thousand acres, from which, under their

management, were shipped large quantities of sugar, and placed the estate in a
position to ship hundreds of tons per year, so that it is to-day one of the great sugar
estates of Natal. While in Natal he was appointed quartermaster of a volunteer company for the protection of the colony against the savages—Kaffers. He visited the
Grequas soon after they first crossed the mountains to No Man's Land, and had some
business with them, and by some suggestions, which they acted upon, averted trouble
between them and the surrounding tribes of savages. From this country he emigrated
to America; married in Nebraska to the oldest daughter of Henry and Martha Smith,
who emigrated to this country from Africa. He was one of the contractors in Echo-
Canon, on the U. P. R. R., under Brigham Young's contract; went to Tintic,
Utah, in 1870, at the opening of that mining district and assisted in laying off and lo-
cating, with A. H. Noon, the present site of Eureka City. He always took much in-
terest in the great iron deposits in that region and, with A. H. Noon, was among the
early locaters there. Since 1876 he became more and more interested in those great
iron deposits and by his continued perseverance succeeded in getting an incorporation
organized with the leading men of Utah County, which was accomplished September
2, 1884. These iron fields bid fair to make of Provo a Pittsburg, for they are inexhaustible and are referred to in this pamphlet elsewhere. Under his management
the first iron plant was made in Utah in commercial quantities and he took the first
into market and sold it. The enterprise is still under his management, as is the Utah.
Valley Iron Mining and Manufacturing Company's properties. With his son, Henry
A. Noon, and Harry Goodwin, he is now carrying on the *American*, a paper devoted
to the mining, manufacturing and the general interests of the country.

grandeur and majesty. Off to the south, over an arm of the
lake, towers Mt. Nebo, at a height of 12,000 feet. It is but a
few miles from the city, and all through the year eternal snow
crowns its sky-embosomed head. The peaks that stand as
ever watchful sentinels to the east of the city, are over 10,000
feet high, and have all the characteristics of the Alps, save
only, it may be, the never departing snows. In the fall of the
year, when the foliage is brightened by the early frosts, they
present that rich picture which makes the mountain home
always the one endearing spot in after life. The beauty of
the autumnal tints everywhere shown in contrast with the
rugged, worn, seared, seamed and scarred visage of the granite
fronts, cliffs and precipices, form a picture too enduring to
fade away from the mind with change of scene and home, as
in softer and milder localities.

The abundance of winged game about Utah Lake in early
days, made it a noted resort for the Ute Indian, after whom,
as already stated, the county and territory seem to have been
named. And it is a pity the other names of springs and creeks
in this lovely basin have not been preserved as well as that of
the "Timpanogas," "Pomountquint," "Waketeke," "Pin-

PROVO ILLUSTRATED. 43

quan," "Pequinnetta." "Petenete," "Pungun," "Watago,"
"Onapah," "Timpah," "Mouna," etc. These have all been
superseded and their memory seems to fast be fading away,
like the races to whom they were first known.

The suburbs of Provo are essentially pastoral in their air,
quiet and pastoral in their surroundings. Here the scene is
such that one weary of life, after searching through all the
world for the rest denied under busier skies, might at last find

JAS. E. DANIELS.

James E. Daniels, son of James Daniels and Elizabeth Salthouse, was born February, 1825, in Manchester, England. He emigrated to the United States in the fall of 1842 with his mother's family, in the ship Medford, and landed at New Orleans. In passing up the river they were ice-bound at St. Louis during the winter. In the spring of 1843 he went to Quincy, Ill., where he had a sister living. From here in 1845 he moved to Nauvoo, where he worked at cabinet making. After the Exodus from Nauvoo he moved back to Quincy, Ill., and fitted out for the trip to Salt Lake Valley. Crossing the Plains in 1850, in Captain Milo Andrus' company, he arrived in Salt Lake City the last of August, of that year. He had married the year previously, and stayed in Salt Lake City until December, when he moved to Utah county and assisted in founding the town of Payson, his being the fourth family that settled at that place. He next moved to Provo City in the fall of 1854, where he has resided until the present time.

He worked at the carpenter business until 1870, when, on the resignation of E. F. Sheets, he was appointed Assessor and Collector for Utah county.

In 1874 he was elected county Recorder, and also county Treasurer, which offices he filled until the year 1882. He was again elected to those offices at the last general election. He also served two terms in the Provo City Council as Alderman, and figured to some extent in the military affairs of the county. He was with General Pace in the Black Hawk war in San Pete, acting as Adjutant on his staff. He served in the famous Echo Canyon Expedition, and was afterward elected Lieutenant-Colonel of the first Regiment of Utah county Militia, under L. John, Nuttall, Colonel. He was commissioned by Governor Durkee, and held that rank when the Utah Militia was disbanded.

some comfort of life, with the promise of peace and freedom that nature holds out in this beautiful region.

The scenery in Provo Canon and, in fact, throughout the different canons that open into this valley of valleys, outrivals that of more famed localities in Colorado. The "Bridal Veil Falls," with their numerous cascades, broken into a gauzy veil as they pour over numberless rocks, until there is left of the stream nothing but the white spray, over which the rainbow tints play wherever the sun strikes it, is pronounced by artists to be among the most beautiful and picturesque bits of scenery which the whole Rocky Mountain region affords; while the grandeur of the canon at the mouth, with its high browed cliffs and deeply-seamed-face, is uneclipsed by and no less impressive than the far-famed "Garden of the Gods." Moreover, the abundance of large game—of deer, of antelope, and of bear—in the mountains will add an additional charm to those who are interested in hunting sports; while the easy distance with which game can be found in this region, robs hunting of the labor that characterizes it elsewhere, and makes it to those who like that sort of recreation, a source of unmixed pleasure.

The climate is equable and bracing during the fall, winter and spring months, while the heat of summer is tempered and its enervating tendencies mitigated by cool winds. The air is invigorating, bracing and wonderfully pure and clear, and the nights, naturally pleasant, are made the more delightful by the night wind which, sweeping from the canons and down the ravines, and in its flight passing over the untrodden snow of ages, refreshes the body and more than compensates for whatever of heat may have been felt during the day.

A bathing resort has already been established on the shores

of the lake, and at a point where the Denver & Rio Grande Railway skirts the edge of the water, a grove of trees has been planted and is in a flourishing condition. The shore and bottom is hard and sandy and is sheltered by a bluff some fifteen feet high, which protects it from the east winds. The temperature of the water is, during the bathing season, warmer than that of the ocean; and the fact that fishing may be indulged in, together with yachting and bathing, will give to Utah Lake an advantage over any other resort in the territory.

HON. JOHN B. MILNER.

Hon. John B. Milner was born at Grindley-on-the-Hill, Nottingham, England, January 27, 1830, and came to Utah in 1853. He received a good education which he improved by persistent application during leisure hours, and which did him excellent service in his subsequent career in the literary and professional world. In 1854 he took up his residence in Provo, which has been his permanent home ever since. For a brief period, after settling in Provo, he was engaged in school teaching, but devoted much of his time to the study of law in which he soon developed both a fondness and aptitude. His subsequent and prominent identification with the bar of Provo brought him before the public in all of the important cases on trial in the local and district courts. In the celebrated trials before Judge Cradlebaugh, Mr. Milner left nothing in doubt as to his ability, and he has ever since been classed among the able lawyers of the Territory, few possessing greater powers of eloquence as a pleader.

At various times during his protracted residence in Provo he has filled the offices of
Internal Revenue Assessor, District, County and City Attorney, Justice of the Peace,
County Assessor and Collector, and has sat in the City Council and in the Territorial
Legislature, where his eloquence as a speaker, received due recognition. Mr. Milner
has also been prominent in the religious affairs of his church and is regarded to-day
as one of the ablest and most eloquent preachers in the Territory.

It demands no unreasonable stretch of the imagination to
picture in the mind's eye an early day when, along the shores
of this lovely stretch of water, for miles and miles, there will
be beautiful drives, handsome villas, surrounded by private
gardens, ornamented and adorned.   And during the summer,
pleasure boats will ply from point to point on the lake ; while
its bosom will be dotted with the white sails of countless
yachts dancing upon its tiny waves.   This, with those rich
and rare sunsets, known only to the Rocky Mountain region,
when the heavens burn with living colors ; when cloud upon
cloud, towering high above each other in the pure atmosphere
seems bent upon destruction ; or, when the rays from the sinking sun melt the mild heavens into the tenderest tints, throwing
a halo of light and radiant glory over the darkening earth—
all, all give that variety so necessary to the soul of him who
loves nature for nature's dear self.

A PROVO MORNING.

The "Industrialist" of Provo has the following co-ming-
ling of the sublime and the ridiculous, which yet tells a tale
of the beauty and loveliness of a morning in this charmed
spot :

Provo has one peculiarity about it, that is not experienced
in any other town along the base of the Wasatch Mountains.
In other climes and in other places twilight begins after sun-
set, but here we have it before sunrise.   At this point of the
range there are no foothills ; no gradual slope, nor benches ;
and Centre Street runs slap up to the big toe of the Wasatch.
On the western side of Utah Lake we see the sunlight on the
peaks of the Oquirrh range, filling its ragged sides with a glow
far beyond the reach of the artist's brush.   But it is yet twilight in Provo for the majestic sun has hours yet in which to
climb up the mighty wall that bound us on the east before he
pokes his head over the summit to bid us good morning.   And

what a morning ! The pines, the massive rocks, the autumn
tinted groves, yawning precipices, the snows of centuries
perched away up amid the clouds ; the awful grandeur of
each intensified in the smiles of the God of day.

It is a scene well worth traveling to behold—well worth
lying over one night in Provo to experience. Old travelers
declare that during the course of their wanderings over the
earth, scenes were encountered that enchanted other senses
besides that of sight. They desired to be alone, for there was
something supernatural in their surroundings and the sound
of a human voice would be sacriligious. We felt that way
upon first beholding a Provo sunrise, and while standing at
the chamber window in the face of nature and the mighty
works of God, there was wonder crept through our heart as
an urchin yelled out from the veranda, "say mister, if yer
want yer breakfast yer got to hustle. The spuds are on the
table an' dad done said grace."

CONCLUSION.

That Provo is destined to be a great city, none who know
her opportunities, or who appreciate the extent of her resources can doubt. The day of her more rapid growth may
be delayed beyond what is now anticipated. We do not think
so. But it will come as sure as the sun is to rise. If the
united effort of all her citizens avail aught; if there be any
teaching in the experience of the past ; if a heaven blessed
country, of boundless mineral resource, and almost limitless
agricultural productions ; if healthful influences and equabili-
ty of climate ; if the greatest of natural attractions give promise of due appreciation, then is Provo destined to become a
city of importance and those who come earliest will be made
most welcome and will participate in the fortune and favors
that await the honest, thrifty and industrious, the health seek-
er and the lover of virtuous pleasures.

www.ingramcontent.com/pod-product-compliance
Lightning Source LLC
Chambersburg PA
CBHW031822090426
42739CB00008B/1368